PENG'S
FUN WITH CHINESE
CHARACTERS
for CHILDREN

Help Your Child Learn Chinese The Fun Way!

 **Marshall Cavendish**
Editions

Other titles by Tan Huay Peng:
Chinese Idioms Vol 1 & 2 • Chinese Radicals Vol 1 & 2 • Hanyu Pinyin • Simplified Chinese Characters • Fun with Chinese Characters Vol 1–3

© 2014 Marshall Cavendish International (Asia) Private Limited
Reprinted 2016

Cover by Benson Tan
Project editors: Thakonrat Hassamon and Justin Lau

Based on the series, *Fun with Chinese Characters, Vol 1–3*

Published by Marshall Cavendish Editions
An imprint of Marshall Cavendish International
1 New Industrial Road, Singapore 536196

Other Marshall Cavendish Offices:
Marshall Cavendish Corporation. 99 White Plains Road, Tarrytown NY 10591-9001, USA • Marshall Cavendish International (Thailand) Co Ltd. 253 Asoke, 12th Flr, Sukhumvit 21 Road, Klongtoey Nua, Wattana, Bangkok 10110, Thailand • Marshall Cavendish (Malaysia) Sdn Bhd, Times Subang, Lot 46, Subang Hi-Tech Industrial Park, Batu Tiga, 40000 Shah Alam, Selangor Darul Ehsan, Malaysia.

Marshall Cavendish is a trademark of Times Publishing Limited

National Library Board, Singapore Cataloguing-in-Publication Data
Chen, Huoping.
Peng's fun with Chinese characters for children : help your child learn Chinese the fun way! / Tan Huay Peng.
-- Singapore : Marshall Cavendish Editions, 2014.
pages cm.
ISBN : 978-981-4561-14-3 (paperback)

1. Chinese characters--Juvenile literature. 2. Chinese language--Writing--Juvenile literature. 3. Chinese language—Etymology--Juvenile literature. I. Title.

PL1171
495.12-- dc23   OCN877845488

Printed in Singapore by Markono Print Media Pte Ltd

Contents

Features of the book

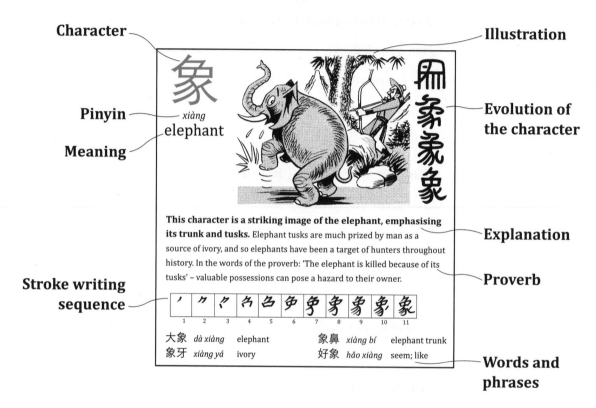

Character

Pinyin

Meaning

象

xiàng
elephant

Illustration

Evolution of the character

This character is a striking image of the elephant, emphasising its trunk and tusks. Elephant tusks are much prized by man as a source of ivory, and so elephants have been a target of hunters throughout history. In the words of the proverb: 'The elephant is killed because of its tusks' – valuable possessions can pose a hazard to their owner.

Explanation

Proverb

Stroke writing sequence

ノ	ク	⼵	⼓	⼱	⼓	⼓	象	象	象	象
1	2	3	4	5	6	7	8	9	10	11

大象 *dà xiàng* elephant   象鼻 *xiàng bí* elephant trunk
象牙 *xiàng yá* ivory   好象 *hǎo xiàng* seem; like

Words and phrases

Introduction to Chinese characters

The Chinese writing system is the oldest in the world that is still being used today. The earliest Chinese characters came into use more than 3000 years ago, during the ancient Shang Dynasty. Some of these characters were simple pictures of things, like ✪ for the sun, and ♒ for water. Others were similar to icons, used to represent more abstract ideas and concepts, like ⊥ for 'up' and ⊤ for 'down'.

These characters did not stay fixed in form. As time went by, they evolved, becoming more stylised and angular. For example, the word for 'sun' developed along these lines: ✪ ⊙ ⊖ ⊟. By around the 5th century, most of the characters arrived at their present form, and stabilised.

This book will first introduce you to some basic principles of Chinese characters, before taking you on a tour of 128 characters, accompanied by illustrations of their origins and their usage. We hope you enjoy this light-hearted take on a fascinating aspect of the Chinese language, and the insight it provides into the Chinese sense of humour. Have fun!

Pictographs
象形字 *(xiàng xíng zì)*

Some of the oldest Chinese characters started out as **pictures** of the things they represent. Such characters are called 'pictographs'. They usually represent the most basic and elemental things known to man, for example:

⊖	日	*rì*	sun		水	水	*shuǐ*	water
☽	月	*yuè*	moon		火	火	*huǒ*	fire
山	山	*shān*	mountain		木	木	*mù*	wood
象	象	*xiàng*	elephant		羊	羊	*yáng*	sheep
耳	耳	*ěr*	ear		目	目	*mù*	eye
口	口	*kǒu*	mouth		手	手	*shǒu*	hand

Ideographs
指事字 *(zhǐ shì zì)*

While pictographs represent pictures, 'ideographs' represent abstract **ideas**. These characters were derived from illustrations of **concepts** rather than objects, for example:

一	*yī*	one
二	*èr*	two
三	*sān*	three
上	*shàng*	up
下	*xià*	down
大	*dà*	big

Compound characters
会意字 *(huì yì zì)*

Some characters were formed by combining two (or more) pictographs or ideographs to suggest **a third meaning**. Examples of such compounds:

木 *mù* wood	+	木 *mù* wood	»	林 *lín* forest
人 *rén* person	+	人 *rén* person	»	从 *cóng* follow
田 *tián* field	+	力 *lì* strength	»	男 *nán* man
女 *nǚ* woman	+	子 *zǐ* child	»	好 *hǎo* good
日 *rì* sun	+	月 *yuè* moon	»	明 *míng* bright

Compound characters (meaning + sound)
形声字 *(xíng shēng zì)*

These are compound characters made up of two distinct parts:

(1) One part suggests the **meaning** of the word. This part is called the '**radical**'. For example, the 氵 radical that represents water is used to form various water-related words like 湿 (*shī*, 'wet') and 海 (*hǎi*, 'sea').

(2) The other part suggests the **sound** of the word. This part is called the '**phonetic**'. For example, 分 (*fēn*) serves as the phonetic component in words like 芬 (*fēn*, 'fragrant'), 粉 (*fěn*, 'powder') and 盆 (*pén*, 'basin').

Radical		Phonetic		Compound
米	+	分	»	粉
mǐ		*fēn*		*fěn*
rice		divide		powder
巾	+	冒	»	帽
jīn		*mào*		*mào*
cloth		risk		hat
心	+	相	»	想
xīn		*xiāng*		*xiǎng*
heart		inspect		think; hope

Traditional and simplified characters
繁体字 *(fán tǐ zì)* / 简体字 *(jiǎn tǐ zì)*

Chinese characters evolved into their modern form by about the 5th century, and have persisted for the most part to today. These are what we call the '**traditional**' characters.

In the 20th century, a major change took place. Many characters were given new forms with fewer strokes. Not all characters were simplified; mostly only the more complicated ones. These '**simplified**' characters are now the standard in most of the Chinese-speaking world, except in Taiwan, Hong Kong and Macau. Examples:

Traditional		Simplified		Method of simplification
雲	»	云	(*yún*, 'cloud')	Omitting a part of the character
門	»	门	(*mén*, 'door')	Omitting some strokes; the simplified form is then also applied when used as a radical
問	»	问	(*wèn*, 'ask')	
網	»	网	(*wǎng*, 'net')	Going back to an ancient form

Character structures
结构 *(jié gòu)*

In a compound character, the component parts can be arranged in various ways within the framework of a square. Here are some basic structures:

Basic Structure	Example	
Left-right	好	(*hǎo*, good)
Top-bottom	胃	(*wèi*, stomach)
Left-middle-right	谢	(*xiè*, thanks)
Top-middle-bottom	意	(*yì*, meaning)
Symmetrical	坐	(*zuò*, sit)

Basic strokes
笔画 *(bǐ huà)*

Stroke	Name of stroke	Direction	Example
一	横 (*héng*) the horizontal stroke	→	王 (*wáng*, king)
丨	竖 (*shù*) the vertical stroke	↓	中 (*zhōng*, middle)
丿	撇 (*piě*) the sweep to the left	↙	才 (*cái*, talent)
㇏	捺 (*nà*) the sweep to the right	↘	尺 (*chǐ*, ruler)
丶	点 (*diǎn*) the dot	↘	下 (*xià*, down)
㇀	提 (*tí*) the upward tick	↗	习 (*xí*, practise)
⅃ ㇁ ㇂	钩 (*gōu*) the hook	↓ → ↙	我 (*wǒ*, me)
㇆	横折 (*héng zhé*) the horizontal turn	㇆	口 (*kǒu*, mouth)
㇄	竖折 (*shù zhé*) the vertical turn	㇄	亡 (*wáng*, perish)

Stroke writing sequence
笔顺 *(bǐ shùn)*

Rule	Example	
Write the **horizontal** stroke, then the **vertical** stroke:	一　十	(*shí*, ten)
Write the strokes in the order from **top to bottom**:	亠　古　京	(*jīng*, capital)
Write the strokes in the order from **left to right**:	丿　川　川	(*chuān*, stream)
Write the **central** component, then the **left and right**:	亅　小　小	(*xiǎo*, small)
Write the **outside** component, then the **inside** components:	丿　几　月	(*yuè*, moon)
Write all the components inside an **enclosure** before sealing it:	丨　冂　国　国	(*guó*, country)

Alphabetical index (by pinyin)

女 *nǚ*
woman

Early pictographs for 'woman' showed her in a bowing position 冉 and, later, in a kneeling position 呂. The modern version 女 looks like a woman taking a big step.

人	女	女
1	2	3

女儿　*nǚ ér*　　daughter   女王　　*nǚ wáng*　　queen
女孩　*nǚ hái*　　girl   女朋友　*nǚ péng yǒu*　girlfriend

子

zǐ

child; son

The early pictograph for 'child' showed a baby with arms and legs outstretched. Over the years, it evolved into one whose legs are bundled in cloth.

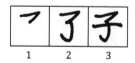

儿子 *ér zi*   son

王子 *wáng zi* prince

子女 *zǐ nǚ*   sons and daughters

子孙 *zǐ sūn*   descendants

好 *hǎo*
good; right

When the character for 'girl'/'daughter' 女 is combined with 子 ('child'/'son'), it forms the character for 'goodness'.

〈	乂	女	女ˊ	好	好
1	2	3	4	5	6

你好 *nǐ hǎo*   Hello
好吃 *hǎo chī*   delicious

好笑 *hǎo xiào*   funny
好听 *hǎo tīng*   pleasant to the ear

3

儿

ér
infant; child　兒 (Traditional)

This character is a pictograph of a growing child – from a crawling infant 𰾯 to a little toddler 兒 with wobbly legs, and to the simplified present form 儿.

儿歌　*ér gē*　nursery rhyme　　孤儿　*gū ér*　orphan
儿童　*ér tóng*　children　　幼儿　*yòu ér*　child; infant

字 *zì*
written word

This character represents a child 子 under a roof 宀, suggesting that the written word is considered as precious as a child.

、	丷	宀	宁	字	字
1	2	3	4	5	6

汉字 *hàn zì* Chinese character   字典 *zì diǎn* dictionary

名字 *míng zì* name   字幕 *zì mù* subtitles

家

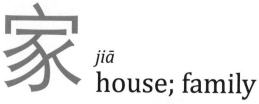

jiā

house; family

A pig 豕 under the roof 宀 represents 'home' 家.

`	八	宀	宀	宀	宇	字	宓	家	家
1	2	3	4	5	6	7	8	9	10

家人	*jiā rén*	one's family	家长	*jiā zhǎng*	parent
家务	*jiā wù*	housework	大家	*dà jiā*	everybody

木

mù

wood

**The word for 'wood' comes from the pictograph of a tree 木,
complete with trunk ↓, branches 一, and roots 八.**

一	十	才	木
1	2	3	4

木工 *mù gōng*   woodwork   木门 *mù mén*   wooden door

木头 *mù tóu*   wooden block   木薯 *mù shǔ*   cassava (tapioca)

lín
woods

When a tree 木 stands next to another tree 木, the new character 林 refers to a group of trees, or the woods. The character made up of three trees 森 represents a forest.

一	十	才	木	朩	村	材	林
1	2	3	4	5	6	7	8

森林 *sēn lín* forest 　　園林 *yuán lín* gardens; park
雨林 *yǔ lín* rainforest 　　林业 *lín yè* forestry

本

běn

root;
origin;
source

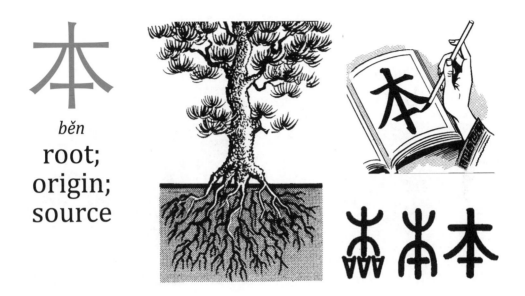

This word for 'root' or 'origin' is a pictograph of a tree with a horizontal line below representing the earth that it is rooted in. The word is also used as a classifier for books, the 'roots' of knowledge.

本来 *běn lái*   originally 本身 *běn shēn* in itself
本地 *běn dì*   local   本子 *běn zi*   notebook

床 *chuáng* bed  牀 (Traditional)

The traditional character for 'bed' was simply a sturdy plank 爿 of wood 木, while the character used today 床 comes from a piece of wood 木 found under a roof 广.

丶	一	广	广	庁	庁	床
1	2	3	4	5	6	7

床单 *chuáng dān*   bedsheet   起床 *qǐ chuáng*   get out of bed
床垫 *chuáng diàn*   mattress   海床 *hǎi chuáng*   sea bed

休

xiū

rest;
cease

This character depicts a person 亻 leaning against a shady tree 木, and means 'rest'. There is a Chinese proverb that says, 'One generation plants the trees under whose shade another generation takes a rest.'

ノ	イ	亻	仁	仈	休
1	2	3	4	5	6

休息 *xiū xi*　　rest; relax

休闲 *xiū xián*　　leisure

休假 *xiū jià*　　go on vacation

退休 *tuì xiū*　　retire

楼

lóu
storey;
building

樓 (Traditional)

In the traditional character, the component 婁 refers to the part of a palace where women 女 were enclosed 中 and confined 毋. The addition of the tree radical 木 suggests a tower as high as a tree and with several floors.

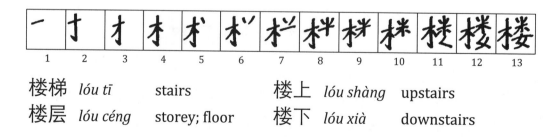

一	寸	才	扌	木	木'	楼	桝	搂	楼	楼	楼
1	2	3	4	5	6	7	8	9	10	11	12	13

楼梯 *lóu tī* stairs   楼上 *lóu shàng* upstairs

楼层 *lóu céng* storey; floor   楼下 *lóu xià* downstairs

草

cǎo
grass

The word for grass combines 屮屮 (a pictograph of blades of grass) with 早 ('morning', suggesting the morning light falling over a field). When used as a radical, the shortened form 艹 is adopted, for example in plant-related words such as 花 (*huā*, 'flower') and 茶 (*chá*, 'tea').

一	十	艹	艹	芇	芇	苩	草	草
1	2	3	4	5	6	7	8	9

草原　*cǎo yuán*　grasslands
花草　*huā cǎo*　flowers and plants

草药　*cǎo yào*　herbal medicine
割草　*gē cǎo*　mow the grass

茶

chá
tea

The tea herb, picked from a tree-like 木 plant 艹, is fermented and dried under cover 𠆢 before being brewed as tea 茶.

一	十	艹	艹	艾	苁	荃	茶	茶
1	2	3	4	5	6	7	8	9

喝茶	*hē chá*	drink tea	茶叶	*chá yè*	tea leaves
茶杯	*chá bēi*	teacup	绿茶	*lǜ chá*	green tea

米

mǐ
rice (uncooked)

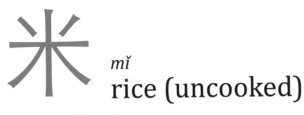

米 is a pictograph of a rice stalk. Its original form showed nine grains of rice ⁛ . This was modified to ⽶ and later became 米, symbolising grains ⅹ that have been separated ➕ after harvesting.

、	〃	丷	半	米	米
1	2	3	4	5	6

米饭	*mǐ fàn*	cooked rice	米色	*mǐ sè*	cream-coloured
米粉	*mǐ fěn*	rice flour	玉米	*yù mǐ*	corn (maize)

15

来

lái

come

來
(Traditional)

Originally a pictograph of wheat or barley, 來 later came to mean 'come'. The simplified form 来 combines rice 米 and tree 木, both of which 'come' from above, in the sense of the proverb: 'He who sows his grain in the field puts his trust in heaven.'

出来 *chū lái*   come out   来回 *lái huí*   make a round trip

来自 *lái zì*   come from   未来 *wèi lái*   the future

 *tián*
field

From dawn to dusk man toiled in the field, and the character he shaped for 'field' was a pictograph of a ploughed field 田.

田地　*tián dì*　farmland　　　耕田　*gēng tián*　to farm
田园　*tián yuán*　fields and gardens　稻田　*dào tián*　paddy field

力

lì
strength

The original form 㑞 was simplified to a graphic image of the forearm 裹 – a potent symbol of physical strength.

| 力量 | *lì liàng* | physical strength | 努力 | *nǔ lì* | work hard |
| 功力 | *gōng lì* | skill | 人力 | *rén lì* | manpower; labour |

男 *nán*
man; male

Exerting strength 力 on a field 田 is the symbol for a man 男.

丨	冂	𠆢	用	田	罗	男
1	2	3	4	5	6	7

男人 *nán rén*   man   男生 *nán shēng*   boy student

男孩 *nán hái*   boy   男性 *nán xìng*   male

里

lǐ
inside;
mile

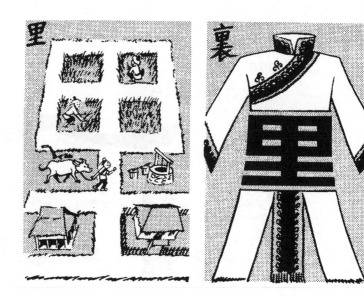

里 represents a village made up of 田 (field) and 土 (earth). The character 里 also means a Chinese mile, a unit of length that is equivalent to about 500 metres – the length of a village.

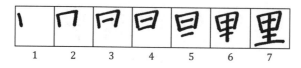

| 里面 | *lǐ miàn* | inside; interior | 公里 | *gōng lǐ* | kilometre |
| 这里 | *zhè lǐ* | here | 家里 | *jiā lǐ* | home |

工 *gōng*
work; labour

工 is a pictograph of the ancient workman's square or carpenter's ruler, and means 'work', 'labour' or 'skill'. In an early form, 𠓗 included three parallel lines marked along the ruler.

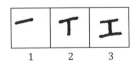

| 工人 | *gōng rén* | worker | 工厂 | *gōng chǎng* | factory |
| 工作 | *gōng zuò* | job; work | 手工 | *shǒu gōng* | handwork |

功

gōng
achievement

Strength 力 put into work 工 gives merit or achievement 功.
On the other hand, little 少 strength 力 results in 劣 (*liè*), which
means 'bad' or 'inferior'.

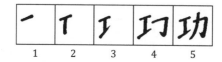

一	丁	工	玎	功
1	2	3	4	5

成功   *chéng gōng*   succeed   功劳   *gōng láo*   contribution

功课   *gōng kè*   homework   功能   *gōng néng*   function

回

huí
return

回 represents curling clouds of smoke or whirlpools in water; or probably an object that rolls; hence the idea of 'returning'.

1	2	3	4	5	6

回家 *huí jiā*   return home   回头 *huí tóu*   turn around

回答 *huí dá*   reply   回想 *huí xiǎng*   recollect

近 *jìn*
near

This ideograph suggests the proper way for a warrior to advance 之 into battle – with battle-axe 斤 in hand – when the battle is upon him. Hence 近, meaning 'near'. The word for 'far' 遠 combines 之 with 袁 – a robe, neccessary for a long journey.

| 附近 | *fù jìn* | nearby | 最近 | *zuì jìn* | recently |
| 靠近 | *kào jìn* | approach; near | 近视 | *jìn shì* | shortsightedness |

日

rì

sun; day

The sun was first represented by a circle with an 'eye' in the centre and rays of light extending to the four corners of the earth ✵. This was simplified to ☉, then ⊖, before finally attaining its present rectangular form 日.

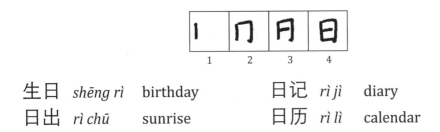

| 生日 | *shēng rì* | birthday | 日记 | *rì jì* | diary |
| 日出 | *rì chū* | sunrise | 日历 | *rì lì* | calendar |

月

yuè

moon; month

The first-known character for moon was a crescent-shaped moon 𝓓 tilting to the right.

月亮　*yuè liàng*　moon

月光　*yuè guāng*　moonlight

新月　*xīn yuè*　crescent moon

月底　*yuè dǐ*　end of the month

明

míng
bright;
brilliant

Man combined two celestial sources of light, the sun 日 and the moon 月, to produce a pictograph for 'bright', 'brilliant' or 'enlightened'.

丨	冂	月	日	日丿	明	明	明
1	2	3	4	5	6	7	8

明亮 *míng liàng* bright   明白 *míng bái* understand

明确 *míng què* clear; definite   明显 *míng xiǎn* obvious

早

zǎo

early; morning

The character for 'early' or 'morning' shows the sun 日 at the height of a man's helmet 十 (the old form of 甲, 'helmet' or 'armour').

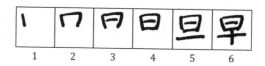

一	冂	冃	日	旦	早
1	2	3	4	5	6

早晨 *zǎo chén* early morning   早操 *zǎo cāo* morning exercise

早饭 *zǎo fàn* breakfast   早日 *zǎo rì* at an early date

东 東 (Traditional)

dōng
east

$$日 + 木 = 東 = 東$$

Man was looking for a suitable character for 'east', the direction he faced when he saw the sun rise every day. One morning he observed the rising sun 日 through the trees 木, and put these components together to form the character 東.

东方 *dōng fāng* the East   中东 *zhōng dōng* Middle East

东边 *dōng biān* east side   东西 *dōng xi* thing

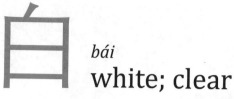

bái

white; clear

As the sun 日 peeps above the horizon, its very first ray ✓ begins
to clear the darkness of night. Hence, 白 is the character for
'clear', 'white' or 'plain'. When paired with 'bright' (明), 明白 means
'clear' or 'understand'.

✓	亻	冂	白	白
1	2	3	4	5

| 白云 | *bái yún* | white cloud | 白糖 | *bái táng* | white sugar |
| 白天 | *bái tiān* | daytime | 白菜 | *bái cài* | Chinese cabbage |

30

春 *chūn* spring

In the early character for 'spring' 萅, man showed the growth and flowering 屯 of plants 艸 in the sun ⊖. Over time, the character was modified to 春.

一	二	三	丰	夫	表	春	春	春
1	2	3	4	5	6	7	8	9

春天	*chūn tiān*	springtime	春雨	*chūn yǔ*	spring rain
春风	*chūn fēng*	spring breeze	春节	*chūn jié*	Chinese New Year

zhōng
centre; middle

By shooting an arrow 丨 into the centre of a square target 口, man scored a bull's-eye, and the character 中 came to mean 'centre'. To this early form, he added four decorative stripes 中, rearranged them 中, stripped them off 中, before finally arriving back at the pure form 中.

、	冂	口	中
1	2	3	4

中午　*zhōng wǔ*　midday　　　中国　*zhōng guó*　China
中心　*zhōng xīn*　centre; hub　　中学　*zhōng xué*　middle school

上

shàng

up; above

Since 'up' and 'down' are abstract terms, man conveyed these ideas graphically by using a simple stroke and a horizontal baseline ▬. The stroke above the baseline was originally a dot 丄, subsequently extended to a line 二, propped upright 丄, and embellished 上. The form used today is 上.

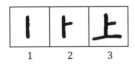

楼上	*lóu shàng*	upstairs	上午	*shàng wǔ*	morning
头上	*tóu shàng*	overhead	上衣	*shàng yī*	upper outer garment

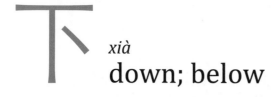 *xià*

down; below

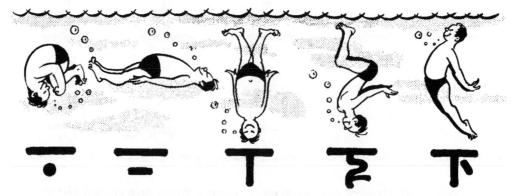

In the character for 'down', the stroke below the horizontal baseline was originally a dot ⼀, which was then extended to a line ⼆ for ease of writing. The modified forms 丅 and 𠄠 eventually led to the present form 下.

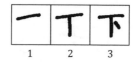

1　2　3

楼下	*lóu xià*	downstairs	下马	*xià mǎ*	dismount a horse
下跌	*xià diē*	fall; tumble	地下	*dì xià*	underground

34

小

xiǎo
small;
young

小 small

大 big

A vertical stroke 丿 separating two little ones 八 gave man his concept of 'small'.

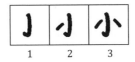

丿	小	小
1	2	3

小孩 *xiǎo hái*	child
小学 *xiǎo xué*	primary school

小吃 *xiǎo chī*	snacks
小姐 *xiǎo jiě*	young lady

 *dà*
big; great

The character for 'big' is simply a man with arms stretched out to the limit 大.

大人	*dà rén*	adult
大小	*dà xiǎo*	size

长大	*zhǎng dà*	grow up
大衣	*dà yī*	overcoat

太

tài

too; over; excessive

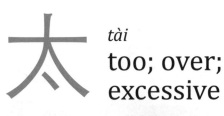

By putting 'big' 大 over a baseline —, man came up with a character 太 meaning 'too much' or 'over the limit'. The line was later modified to a teeny-weeny stroke 太.

一	丆	大	太
1	2	3	4

太多 *tài duō* too many 太空 *tài kōng* outer space

太少 *tài shǎo* too few/little 太太 *tài tai* wife; madam

天

tiān
sky;
heaven;
day

The character for 'sky' is a stylised representation of a man 人 extending his arms 大 under the heavens 天. The character also means 'day'.

一	二	千	天
1	2	3	4

蓝天 *lán tiān*   blue sky

今天 *jīn tiān*   today

昨天 *zuó tiān*   yesterday

天天 *tiān tiān*   everyday

人 *rén*

person; human

The first-known character for 'man' shows a person with head, hands and legs 𝒴. It later became a two-stroke character to show a person standing with legs apart 人.

ノ	人
1	2

工人   *gōng rén*   worker   人品   *rén pǐn*   personal character

好人   *hǎo rén*   good person   人造   *rén zào*   man-made

从

cóng
follow;
from

從
(Traditional)

The traditional form 從 represents two men 从 walking 彳 and stopping 止. The simplified form shows one man following another man 从.

跟从　*gēn cóng*　　follow behind　　从小　*cóng xiǎo*　from childhood

服从　*fú cóng*　　follow an order　　从头　*cóng tóu*　from the beginning

40

zhòng

crowd; many

(Traditional)

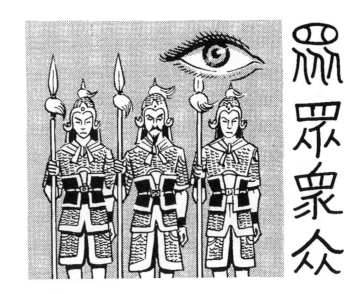

An early form 眾 showed three or many persons 从 as seen by the eye 罒. It was modified to 眾, and then to 众 – three persons, representing a crowd.

ノ	人	仒	众	夵	众
1	2	3	4	5	6

众多 *zhòng duō* numerous   观众 *guān zhòng* spectators

大众 *dà zhòng* the public   出众 *chū zhòng* stand out

坐 *zuò*
sit

The ideograph for 'sit' shows two men talking face-to-face 人人 while sitting on the ground 土.

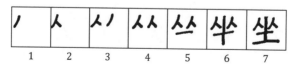

ノ	人	人ノ	从	丛	坐	坐
1	2	3	4	5	6	7

请坐　*qǐng zuò*　Please have a seat.　　静坐　*jìng zuò*　meditate

坐下　*zuò xià*　sit down　　　　　　坐车　*zuò chē*　go by car/vehicle

伞

săn
umbrella

伞
(Traditional)

Early forms of the pictograph for 'umbrella' 伞 show four people 仌仌 taking shelter under it. In the simplified form, however, the people have disappeared, leaving just the umbrella itself 伞.

雨伞 *yŭ săn*	umbrella	竹伞 *zhú săn*	bamboo umbrella
阳伞 *yáng săn*	parasol	带伞 *dài săn*	bring an umbrella

老

lǎo
old

The early character for 'old' 耂 combined 毛 (hair), 人 (person) and 匕 (change). When the hair of a person changes colour and turns gray or white, it is a sign of old age. Over time, the character evolved into its present form 老.

一	十	土	步	步	老
1	2	3	4	5	6

古老	*gǔ lǎo*	ancient	老师	*lǎo shī*	teacher
老人	*lǎo rén*	old person	老板	*lǎo bǎn*	boss

我

wǒ

I; me

The early form of this word shows two spears crossed against each other 𢦔. It was later modified to 我, a pictograph of a hand 手 grasping a spear 戈. When man wields a spear, his ego emerges. Hence 我: I.

ノ	一	手	手	扑	我	我
1	2	3	4	5	6	7

我的   *wǒ de*   my; mine   自我   *zì wǒ*   self- ; oneself

我们   *wǒ men*   we; us   忘我   *wàng wǒ*   selfless

mén
door;
gate

門

(Traditional)

Just as 戶 symbolises a single door, so 門 represents a double door. In its present form, 門 has been simplified to an open doorway 门.

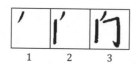

′	｜′	｜′
1	2	3

大门   *dà mén*   main door   出门   *chū mén*   go out

门口   *mén kǒu*   doorway   门票   *mén piào*   admission ticket

mén; men

plural
sign

們

(Traditional)

This character, which combines 人 (person) and 門 (double door), is the plural sign applied to people and pronouns.

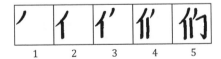

人们 *rén men*　people; the public　　你们 *nǐ men*　you (plural)

我们 *wǒ men*　we; us　　　　　　　他们 *tā men*　they; them

问

wèn

ask

問

(Traditional)

Enquiries are often made at the door, the entrance to a house. A mouth 口 at the door 門 forms the character for 'ask' or 'enquire' 問. It can also mean 'question'.

'	⺆	门	问	问	问
1	2	3	4	5	6

问题 *wèn tí*   question; problem   问答 *wèn dá*   question and answer

问号 *wèn hào*   question mark   问好 *wèn hǎo*   send one's regards

耳 *ěr*
ear

The pictograph that man created for the listening ear began with a natural form 𝕰 and evolved gradually into a stylised version 耳. Man knows the wisdom of listening, and there is a proverbial saying: 'A good talker is inferior to a good listener.'

一	丁	丌	开	耳	耳
1	2	3	4	5	6

耳朵 *ěr duo* ear
耳环 *ěr huán* earrings

耳机 *ěr jī* earphone
顺耳 *shùn ěr* pleasing to the ear

49

闻
wén
hear
聞 (Traditional)

In this ideograph, 'ear' 耳 becomes 'hear' 聞 when placed at the door 門. By extension, 聞 also means 'news', as the ear is the door to information.

1	2	3	4	5	6	7	8	9

新闻　*xīn wén*　news　　传闻　*chuán wén*　rumour
闻人　*wén rén*　famous person　见闻　*jiàn wén*　knowledge

50

开

kāi
open

開
(Traditional)

A bar or bolt ⼀ across the door 門 means 'to shut' 閂.
Two hands 廾 taking away the bar ⼀ signifies 'to open' 開.

1   2   3   4

开门	*kāi mén*	open the door	开始	*kāi shǐ*	start
开花	*kāi huā*	to blossom	开车	*kāi chē*	drive a car

雨

yǔ
rain

**The character for rain 雨 is a picture of raindrops ⸬ falling |
from a cloud 冂 in the heavens ⼀.**

| | 雨季 | *yǔ jì* | rainy season | 雨天 | *yǔ tiān* | rainy day |
| 雨伞 | *yǔ sǎn* | umbrella | 雨衣 | *yǔ yī* | raincoat |

电

diàn
electricity;
lightning

電
(Traditional)

The symbols for 'rain' 雨 and 'lightning' 电 when combined came to represent 'lightning' as well as 'electricity'. This was later simplified to 电.

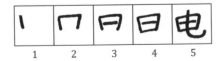

电话 *diàn huà* telephone   雷电 *léi diàn* thunder and lightning
电脑 *diàn nǎo* computer   电影 *diàn yǐng* movie

云

yún
cloud

雲

(Traditional)

When warm vapours (⺞ or ㄙ) rise (上 or ⼆) and reach the colder regions of the atmosphere, they condense and form clouds 云. Loading the clouds with rain 雨 produces the traditional character 雲. The simplified version relieves the clouds of their load, going back to its original form 云.

| 多云 | *duō yún* | cloudy | 云层 | *yún céng* | layers of cloud |
| 乌云 | *wū yún* | dark clouds | 星云 | *xīng yún* | nebula |

yáng
sheep;
goat

Early pictographs of the sheep/goat show frontal views of the head; later versions had horns, ears, legs and tail added. When combined with other components, the tail is often left out: ⅄.

ヽ	⅄	⅀	㇒	㇒	羊
1	2	3	4	5	6

绵羊 *mián yáng* sheep 羊毛 *yáng máo* wool

山羊 *shān yáng* goat 羊肉 *yáng ròu* mutton; lamb

美

měi
beautiful

大 originally represented a person grown big; the lamb 羊 is admired for its peace-loving virtue. A mature person who has the gentle disposition of a lamb is regarded as beautiful and admirable: 美.

美女	*měi nǚ*	beautiful lady	美好	*měi hǎo*	fine; happy
美术	*měi shù*	fine arts	美国	*měi guó*	America

刀

dāo
knife

This character is a pictograph of a knife or sword. A sharp blade is likened to a person who has too much power, and a proverb warns: 'A knife that's too sharp easily cuts the fingers.'

| 刀叉 | *dāo chā* | knife and fork | 剪刀 | *jiǎn dāo* | scissors |
| 刀具 | *dāo jù* | cutting tool | 开刀 | *kāi dāo* | perform surgery |

八

bā
eight

The original meaning of 八, which was made up of two separate strokes, was to divide or to separate. Probably because the number 8 can be easily divided and subdivided, 八 came to stand for 8, and in fact the original form was made up of eight strokes.

| 八百 | *bā bǎi* | eight hundred | 八月 | *bā yuè* | August |
| 第八 | *dì bā* | eighth | 八爪鱼 | *bā zhǎo yú* | octopus |

58

分

fēn

divide;
separate

The ideograph 分 combines 八 (divide) with 刀 (knife) to convey the concept of cutting, dividing or separating. The word is also used to mean any small division, component or part, e.g., a minute, a mark or a cent.

ノ	八	分	分
1	2	3	4

分开 *fēn kāi*   separate   分钟 *fēn zhōng*   a minute
分散 *fēn sàn*   scatter   公分 *gōng fēn*   centimetre

粉

fěn
powder

Face powder in China was once made by grinding rice into fine particles. Hence the ideograph 粉 for face powder – from 米 (rice) and 分 (divide; break down). The word now refers to all types of powder, not just the cosmetic variety.

| 粉笔 | *fěn bǐ* | blackboard chalk | 玉米粉 | *yù mǐ fěn* | corn flour |
| 粉碎 | *fěn suì* | crush | 粉红 | *fěn hóng* | pink |

火 *huǒ*
fire

火 is a pictograph of 'fire', produced by rubbing two stones together.

㇀	㇀㇀	㇀㇀	火
1	2	3	4

点火   *diǎn huǒ*   light a fire   火车   *huǒ chē*   train

火柴   *huǒ chái*   match   火箭   *huǒ jiàn*   rocket

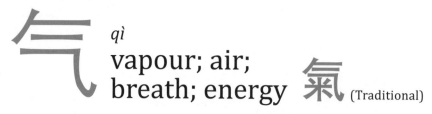

気 *qì*
vapour; air;
breath; energy 氣 (Traditional)

The ancient form ⿰ showed the sun ☉ and fire 火 heating water into vapour ⸙. Over time, the character came to depict vapour 气 rising from boiling rice 米; this developed into the traditional form 氣.

ノ	⺦	⺣	⺣	气
1	2	3	4	5

气球　*qì qiú*　balloon　　　生气　*shēng qì*　angry

气温　*qì wēn*　air temperature　断气　*duàn qì*　draw a last breath

光 *guāng*
bright; light

The ancient form 炗 represents the light of twenty 廿 fires 火.
The modern form 光 portrays a man 儿 bearing a torch 火.

Whatever the form, 光 means brightness and glory which, unfortunately, never lasts. Hence: 'A bright dawn does not always make a fine day.'

丨	丬	屮	半	光	光
1	2	3	4	5	6

阳光 *yáng guāng* sunlight   光彩 *guāng cǎi* radiance; glory

月光 *yuè guāng* moonlight   光滑 *guāng huá* glossy

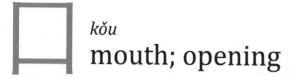 *kǒu*
mouth; opening

The first-known character for mouth was a pictograph of an open mouth ⩛, which became a smile ⩜, before finally settling on the present squarish form 口. By extension, 口 also means an opening.

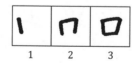

口红 *kǒu hóng*   lipstick   出口 *chū kǒu*   exit; way out
口水 *kǒu shuǐ*   saliva   口袋 *kǒu dài*   pocket

64

土 *tǔ* earth

Man has always depended on the earth for subsistence. In writing, earth is represented by its two layers 二 (the topsoil and subsoil) from which plants sprout Ⅰ, hence 土.

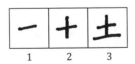

一	十	土
1	2	3

泥土　*ní tǔ*　soil; clay
土地　*tǔ dì*　land; field

国土　*guó tǔ*　country's territory
土豆　*tǔ dòu*　potato

吐

tǔ
spit out

tù
vomit

The ideograph 吐, literally 'from mouth 口 to earth 土', means to spit or throw up. Figuratively, it means to disclose or reveal the truth – like spilling the beans or letting the cat out of the bag. In this sense, beware: 'A very big secret can be hurled out of a little mouth.'

吐痰 *tǔ tán*   expectorate   吐露 *tǔ lù*   disclose; reveal
吐气 *tǔ qì*   blow off steam   呕吐 *ǒu tù*   vomit

66

右

yòu
right

The character for 'right' is simply a hand 𠂇 and a mouth 口, signifying the hand you eat with – the right.

1 2 3 4 5

右边 *yòu biān*	right side	左右 *zuǒ yòu*	approximately
右手 *yòu shǒu*	right hand	座右铭 *zuò yòu míng*	motto

叫 *jiào*
call

呼唷叫叫

The word for 'call' has its roots in the marketplace: 叫 means to call out 口 the measure 斗 (which is from an earlier form 𣁳, a measuring ladle 𠂌 with ten 十).

l	ㄇ	口	叮	叫
1	2	3	4	5

呼叫 *hū jiào* call out; shout   叫醒 *jiào xǐng* wake someone up
叫好 *jiào hǎo* cheer; applaud   尖叫 *jiān jiào* scream

唱

chàng
sing

The 昌 radical is composed of 日 (sun) and 曰 (speak), meaning 'prosperous' or 'splendid', just as the sun sends forth rays and the mouth puts forth words. Combined with the mouth radical 口, 唱 means 'sing'.

丶	冂	口	口'	口冂	口月	口日	唱	唱	唱	唱
1	2	3	4	5	6	7	8	9	10	11

唱歌	*chàng gē*	sing (a song)	合唱	*hé chàng*	chorus
演唱	*yǎn chàng*	perform a song	唱片	*chàng piàn*	music record

说

shuō
speak

說
(Traditional)

说 is a character that speaks for itself. It means to speak, i.e., to exchange 兑 words 言. It is an ideograph of an elder brother 兄 separating his words 八, exchanging them in speech 说. It can also mean 'theory', 'opinion' or 'story'.

、	讠	讠	讠	讠	讠	说	说	说
1	2	3	4	5	6	7	8	9

说明   *shuō míng*   explain   听说   *tīng shuō*   be told; hear of
说谎   *shuō huǎng*   tell a lie   小说   *xiǎo shuō*   novel

信

xìn
believe;
trust;
letter

This character depicts a man 人 standing by his word 言, a fitting symbol for faith and trust. As only man can transmit his word by writing, 信 also means the written letter.

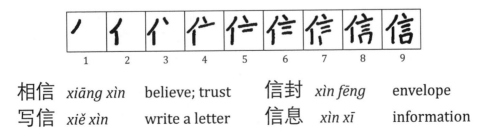

ノ	イ	亻	仁	信	信	信	信	信
1	2	3	4	5	6	7	8	9

相信	*xiāng xìn*	believe; trust
写信	*xiě xìn*	write a letter

信封	*xìn fēng*	envelope
信息	*xìn xī*	information

渴

kě

thirsty

The phonetic 曷 originally meant 'to ask' – a beggar 匃 who speaks 曰. 匃 itself means a wanderer 勹 who seeks to enter 入 a refuge ㇄. 曰 is a mouth 口 with word 一. When you ask 曷 for water 氵 you must be thirsty: 渴.

`	丶	氵	氵	沪	沪	沪	沪	渇	渇	渇	渴
1	2	3	4	5	6	7	8	9	10	11	12

口渴　*kǒu kě*　feel thirsty　　渴望　*kě wàng*　desire; yearn for
解渴　*jiě kě*　quench one's thirst　渴睡　*kě shuì*　feel sleepy

72

舌

shé
tongue

Early forms of the character show a forked tongue thrust viciously out of the mouth 舌. Over time, it smoothened 舌 and straightened 舌, finally arriving at its present form 舌. 'The tongue is like a sharp knife; it kills without drawing blood' – so warns the Chinese proverb.

舌头	*shé tou*	tongue	舌战	*shé zhàn*	battle of wits
舌尖	*shé jiān*	tip of the tongue	结舌	*jié shé*	tongue-tied

话

huà
speech;
language

話
(Traditional)

Man combined 言 (words) and 舌 (tongue) to produce 話, meaning 'speech' or 'language'. To emphasise the importance of caution against careless speech, the Chinese proverb warns: 'Water and words are easy to pour out but impossible to recover.'

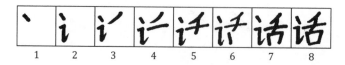

| 对话 | *duì huà* | dialogue | 听话 | *tīng huà* | obedient |
| 会话 | *huì huà* | conversation | 实话 | *shí huà* | truth |

哭

kū

cry; wail

The character 哭 uses two mouths 吅 to express intense crying, like the wailing of dogs 犬. Two mouths may effectively express crying and howling, but certainly, 'two buckets of tears,' according to the proverb, 'will not heal a bruise.'

ˋ	冖	口	叮	叮	吅	哭	哭	哭	哭
1	2	3	4	5	6	7	8	9	10

哭泣 *kū qì*　　weep　　　　　　　　　痛哭 *tòng kū*　wail bitterly
哭诉 *kū sù*　　complain tearfully　　哭喊 *kū hǎn*　cry and shout

笑

xiào
laugh

笑 has an amusing origin. The phonetic element 夭 depicts a man 大 inclining his head ノ to laugh more easily. The bamboo radical ⺮ likens such laughter to the swaying of bamboo in the breeze. But laughing or smiling is serious business, as implied in the proverb: 'A man without a smiling face should not open a shop.'

ノ	⺊	⺺	灯	灯	⺮	竺	竺	笔	笑
1	2	3	4	5	6	7	8	9	10

好笑 *hǎo xiào* funny   微笑 *wēi xiào* smile
笑口 *xiào kǒu* smiling mouth   笑话 *xiào huà* joke

shǒu

hand

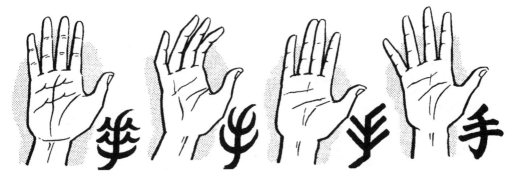

The earliest pictograph for 'hand' 龙 focused on the lines of the palm, but later focused on the five fingers 火. From there, the fingers were straightened out, and the character eventually took on the modern form 手.

| 手表 | *shǒu biǎo* | wrist-watch | 手巾 | *shǒu jīn* | hand towel |
| 手臂 | *shǒu bì* | arm | 放手 | *fàng shǒu* | let go |

友

yǒu
friend

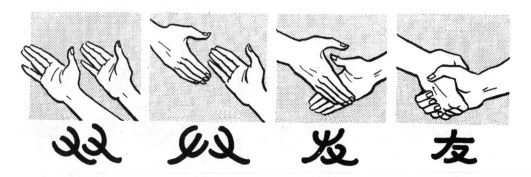

The character for 'friend' originated with two right hands 双双, that later reached out to clasp each other in friendship 双双. By placing the hands one upon the other 双, the modern form 友 was arrived at.

| 朋友 | *péng you* | friend | 友情 | *yǒu qíng* | friendship |
| 交友 | *jiāo yǒu* | make friends | 网友 | *wǎng yǒu* | internet friend |

有

yǒu

have

Early forms portrayed a hand 彐 holding a piece of meat 𠬛,
signifying possession 㝵. Because of the resemblance between
meat 𠬛 and moon 月, man soon lost sight of meat and reached for the
moon, promising it to anyone he wished to possess.

一	ナ	才	冇	有	有
1	2	3	4	5	6

没有 *méi yǒu*   have not   有名 *yǒu míng*   well-known
有力 *yǒu lì*   strong; powerful 有用 *yǒu yòng*   useful

肉

ròu
meat

This character is drawn from pieces of dried meat 仌 wrapped in a bundle 冂. From the ancient custom of offering such dried meat to one's teachers came the term 'dried-meat money' – a teacher's pay.

| 猪肉 | *zhū ròu* | pork | 羊肉 | *yáng ròu* | mutton |
| 牛肉 | *niú ròu* | beef | 肉丸 | *ròu wán* | meatballs |

丝

sī

silk

絲
(Traditional)

The silk radical 糸 comes from an older form 𢆶, representing two cocoons 𢆶 over the twisting of several strands into a single thread 小. The radical is then repeated 絲, indicating that many threads are required to form silk. In the modern simplified version, the two components are woven together to give 丝.

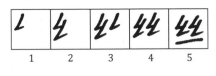

| 丝绸 | *sī chóu* | silk cloth | 丝带 | *sī dài* | silk ribbon |
| 丝织 | *sī zhī* | silk weaving | 铁丝 | *tiě sī* | wire |

81

给

gěi

give;
provide

給
(Traditional)

Gifts promote harmony 合 **between friends and relatives; and
what better present to give than silk** 糸**, a material appreciated
by all. Hence** 給**, meaning 'to give'.** The practice of giving brings
blessings, for there is more happiness in giving than there is in receiving.

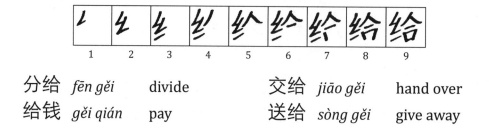

| 分给 | *fēn gěi* | divide | 交给 | *jiāo gěi* | hand over |
| 给钱 | *gěi qián* | pay | 送给 | *sòng gěi* | give away |

山 *shān*
mountain

A mountain range, with three peaks, forms the pictograph for 'mountain' or 'hill' 山.

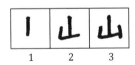

1   2   3

高山 *gāo shān* high mountain   上山 *shàng shān* go up the hill

火山 *huǒ shān* volcano   下山 *xià shān* come down the hill

shí
stone

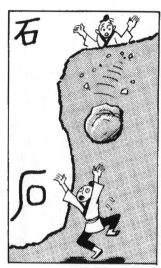

The word for 'stone' is a picture of a rock 口 falling from a cliff 厂. A related word is 岩 (*yán*), which refers to a steep rock formation 石 that looks like a hill 山. The rock, being strong, symbolises integrity. Hence: 'Slander cannot destroy an honest man; when the flood recedes the rock appears.'

一	丁	丆	石	石
1	2	3	4	5

宝石 *bǎo shí*   gemstone   钻石 *zuàn shí*   diamond
石油 *shí yóu*   petroleum; oil 化石 *huà shí*   fossil

高

gāo
high; tall

The character for 'high' is a pictograph of a tall tower or pavilion 亩 standing on a raised structure 冂 with a hall 口.

When it comes to position, no person stoops so low as the one most eager to rise high in the world. But beware: 'He who climbs too high will have a heavy fall.'

丶	亠	亠	宁	古	户	高	高	高	高
1	2	3	4	5	6	7	8	9	10

高级 *gāo jí* high-level 身高 *shēn gāo* height
高楼 *gāo lóu* tall building 高兴 *gāo xìng* glad; happy

鸟

niǎo
bird

鳥
(Traditional)

In its traditional form, 鳥 is a picture of a long-tailed bird, showing off its beauty and enjoying its freedom. Unfortunately, beauty has not always been an asset to the bird for, as the saying goes, 'It's the beautiful bird that we put in the cage.' The simplified form 鸟 sees the poor bird stripped of its feathers.

| 小鸟 | *xiǎo niǎo* | little bird | 鸟笼 | *niǎo lóng* | birdcage |
| 鸟巢 | *niǎo cháo* | bird's nest | 鸟食 | *niǎo shí* | bird food |

86

岛 *dǎo* island 島 (Traditional)

Sea-birds often nest on rock outcrops in the sea. Hence a bird 鳥 over a mountain 山 gave the concept for island 島. The ancient form showed a bird hovering over a mountain, with feet visible 㠀. As the character evolved, the bird settled on the mountain 島, its feet now hidden, and hence probably hatching the simplified character: 岛.

勹	勽	鸟	岛	岛	岛
1	2	3	4	5	6

半岛   *bàn dǎo*   peninsula   群岛   *qún dǎo*   group of islands

岛国   *dǎo guó*   island nation   冰岛   *bīng dǎo*   Iceland

竹

zhú

bamboo

Originally written as 个个, the character for bamboo is a pictograph of two whorls of bamboo leaves. Unlike a wayward man, the bamboo grows straight and upright into a useful and decorative plant. 'The bamboo stick makes a good child,' says the proverb.

ノ	𠂉	𠂉	𠂆	𠂉	竹
1	2	3	4	5	6

竹林　*zhú lín*　　bamboo forest　　　竹笋　*zhú sǔn*　　bamboo shoot

竹竿　*zhú gān*　　bamboo pole　　　　竹纸　*zhú zhǐ*　　bamboo paper

书

shū

book;
writings

書

(Traditional)

書 **is the product of a pen** 聿 **that speaks** 曰**, i.e., books and writings.** The radical 聿 itself comes from a stylus ｜ in hand ⺕ scratching a line 一 on a tablet 一; while 曰 is the mouth ⼝ with a word in it. Because not everything the pen speaks is truth, 'It is better to have no books than to rely blindly on them.'

| 1 | 2 | 3 | 4 |

| 读书 *dú shū* | to study | 书店 *shū diàn* | bookshop |
| 书包 *shū bāo* | bookbag | 书法 *shū fǎ* | calligraphy |

毛

máo

hair; fur

毛 **is a pictograph of the hair of man or beast.** Our hairs may not be numbered but, says the proverb: 'Pull a hair and the whole body may be affected.'

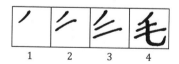

羊毛 *yáng máo*	lambswool	毛笔 *máo bǐ*	writing brush
毛巾 *máo jīn*	towel	毛病 *máo bìng*	fault; problem

笔
bǐ
pen;
writing brush 筆 (Traditional)

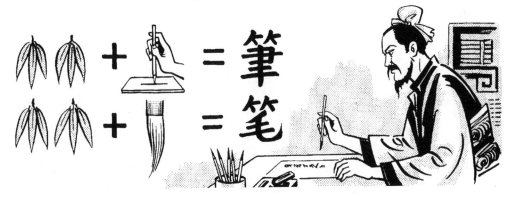

A hand ⺕ holding a tool ｜, scratching lines ⼀ on a tablet ⼀,
represents a writing stylus 聿. Bamboo ⺮ added to the stylus
produces 'pen' 筆. The word can also be written as 笔, a
combination of bamboo ⺮ and brush hair 毛.

ノ	⺮	⺮	⺮	⺮	⺮	⺮	笁	笔	笔
1	2	3	4	5	6	7	8	9	10

铅笔　*qiān bǐ*　pencil　　　笔名　*bǐ míng*　pen name
笔画　*bǐ huà*　writing strokes　下笔　*xià bǐ*　set down on paper

水

shuǐ
water

Water, a natural source of power, is represented by a pictograph of a surging river and four whirls 水. A variant form, using only three drops 氵, is the radical in 'watery' words such as 河 (*hé*, 'river') and 海 (*hǎi*, 'sea').

喝水　*hē shuǐ*　drink water
河水　*hé shuǐ*　river water

水瓶　*shuǐ píng*　water bottle
水果　*shuǐ guǒ*　fruits

hǎi

sea; ocean

母 is a picture of a woman with breasts for suckling a child, signifying mother 毝. 每 compares a mother 母 with a sprout 乀, always reproducing; hence meaning 'every', 'always'. 海 represents the sea, where there is always 每 plenty of water 氵.

丶	丶丶	氵	氵	氵⁻	汒	海	海	海	海
1	2	3	4	5	6	7	8	9	10

海滩 *hǎi tān* beach   海豚 *hǎi tún* dolphin
海外 *hǎi wài* overseas   海鲜 *hǎi xiān* seafood

93

冰

bīng
ice

The radical 冫 shows water dripping and is added to 水 (water) to freeze it into ice: 冰. The illustration contrasts icy coldness with fiery passion.

丶	冫	刁	冫	冰	冰
1	2	3	4	5	6

冰冻　*bīng dòng*　freeze   冰山　*bīng shān*　iceberg

冰块　*bīng kuài*　ice-cube   冰箱　*bīng xiāng*　refrigerator

目 *mù*
eye

In its early form, the character for 'eye' was drawn with eyelids and pupil 👁. When stylised as ⬜, it looked too similar to ▦ ('four'); so it was stood on end 🄴 and finally squared off 目. It would seem that even with his very own eyes, man could not see eye to eye.

| 目光 | *mù guāng* | vision; view | 目前 | *mù qián* | at present |
| 盲目 | *máng mù* | blind; aimless | 目的 | *mù dì* | purpose; aim |

见 *jiàn*
see 見 (Traditional)

For the verb 'to see', the eye 目 was set atop man 人 . As the eye grew, man shrank, producing 見, now simplified to 见.

丨	冂	𠃌	见
1	2	3	4

不见 *bú jiàn* lost; disappeared 见面 *jiàn miàn* meet someone

常见 *cháng jiàn* common 再见 *zài jiàn* See you again

看

kàn
look

In this ideograph, man raised his hand 手 above his eyes 目 to cut off the sun's rays in order to see clearly 看.

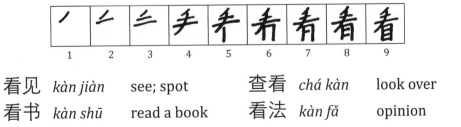

| 看见 | *kàn jiàn* | see; spot | 查看 | *chá kàn* | look over |
| 看书 | *kàn shū* | read a book | 看法 | *kàn fǎ* | opinion |

miàn
face

This character combines 囗 (an outline of the face) with 百 (head), featuring the eyes 目 as its most prominent part. Because a person is identified by his face, we know a man's face, not his mind. Nevertheless, 'Be able to say to his face what you say behind his back.'

| 面前 | *miàn qián* | in front of | 方面 | *fāng miàn* | aspect |
| 面子 | *miàn zi* | face; reputation | 对面 | *duì miàn* | opposite |

98

帽 *mào* hat

A hat is made with the cloth radical 巾 combined with the phonetic 冒 (*mào*). By itself 冒 means reckless, or acting with one's eyes 目 covered 冃. Indeed, a cap does not always fit the head of the wearer because 'many a good man can be found under a shabby hat.'

丨	冂	巾	巾′	巾冂	巾冃	帽	帽	帽	帽	帽	帽
1	2	3	4	5	6	7	8	9	10	11	12

帽子　*mào zi*　hat; cap 　　　游泳帽　*yóu yǒng mào*　swimming cap
草帽　*cǎo mào*　straw hat 　　　安全帽　*ān quán mào*　safety helmet

布

bù
cloth

This character combines the radical for 'cloth' 巾 with the phonetic 父 (*fù*). 父 in turn means 'father', and was formerly written as 𠂒, which depicts the right hand 彐 holding the rod of authority |, suggesting discipline, control and order.

一	ナ	㐅	右	布
1	2	3	4	5

棉布　*mián bù*　cotton cloth 布置　*bù zhì*　arrange

桌布　*zhuō bù*　tablecloth 发布　*fā bù*　release; publish

带

dài
strap;
to bring

帶
(Traditional)

This pictograph, meaning a strap of cloth, shows a girdle, with trinkets hanging from it 卅, worn over robes 帀 (two 巾, one over the other). By extension, 帶 also means to 'bring' or 'take along', as articles are often carried, tucked into or worn at the girdle.

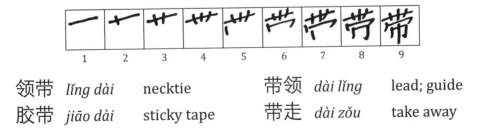

一	十	卄	卅	卅	芇	芇	芇	带
1	2	3	4	5	6	7	8	9

领带　*lǐng dài*　necktie
胶带　*jiāo dài*　sticky tape

带领　*dài lǐng*　lead; guide
带走　*dài zǒu*　take away

夕

xī
evening

夕 **is a picture of the crescent moon appearing on the horizon at dusk, its lower part obstructed by a mountain. Hence the extended meaning: dusk, evening.** To man, the rising moon presents opportunities, but the proverb laments: 'How seldom in life is the moon directly overhead!'

夕阳　*xī yáng*　sunset
朝夕　*zhāo xī*　overnight

前夕　*qián xī*　eve; the day before
除夕　*chú xī*　New Year's Eve

 *duō*

many; much

From morning to evening man toiled in the field, and evening 夕 after evening 夕 he noted the results of his labour. 'Many evenings' 多 soon came to mean 'many'. His hard work bore much 多 fruit 果, producing a new word 夥 (*huǒ*, 'fruitful'), and demonstrating the principle: 'Sow much, reap much; sow little, reap little.'

| 许多 | *xǔ duō* | many | 多谢 | *duō xiè* | Many thanks |
| 多少 | *duō shǎo* | amount; how much | 多余 | *duō yú* | unnecessary |

míng
name

In the dusk 夕, man cannot be seen clearly, so he identifies himself aloud, announcing by mouth 口 his name: 名. And if he has a good name and reputation, he has nothing to fear. Let him draw courage from the saying: 'Travelling or at home, the gentleman does not change his name.'

| 姓名 | *xìng míng* | full name | 名人 | *míng rén* | famous person |
| 名称 | *míng chēng* | name; title | 名词 | *míng cí* | noun |

车

chē
car

车
(Traditional)

This character is a picture of a cart seen from above, its body
日 **and two wheels = connected by an axle ⌡.** The early forms of
車 are as varied as carts, carriages and chariots. But, whatever the form,
where there is a cart in front there is a track behind, so: 'Take warning
from the wrecked cart ahead of you.'

| 1 | 2 | 3 | 4 |

汽车　*qì chē*　　motorcar　　　　车门　*chē mén*　car door
车费　*chē fèi*　　bus/train fare　　火车　*huǒ chē*　train

心

xīn
heart

The original pictograph represented the physical heart, with its sac pulled apart ཡ, and the aorta (main blood vessel) leading away from its base ཡ. A stylisation ཡ provided the basis for the modern form 心. Recognising this vital organ's role as the seat of motivation for both good and evil, man takes to heart the ancient saying: 'Honey mouth, dagger heart.'

| 人心 | *rén xīn* | human heart | 心情 | *xīn qíng* | state of mind |
| 开心 | *kāi xīn* | happy; glad | 中心 | *zhōng xīn* | centre |

爱

ài

love

愛

(Traditional)

The traditional 愛 is made up of ㅆ (breathe into), 心 (heart) and 夂 (gracious motion), implying that what gives breath to the heart and inspires gracious motion is love – an idealistic love. The simplifed form 爱 highlights the role of friendship 友 (hand ナ in hand 又) – a more realistic love.

| 母爱 | mǔ ài | maternal love | 爱人 | ài rén | sweetheart; lover |
| 爱好 | ài hào | interest; hobby | 可爱 | kě ài | cute |

想

xiǎng
think

The phonetic component 相 represents an eye 目 behind a tree 木 on the lookout for possible danger, and signifies 'to examine'. Combining this with the heart/mind radical 心 produces 想, meaning to examine or inspect one's heart or mind, i.e., to think, ponder or hope.

一	十	才	木	术	机	机	相	相	相	想	想	想
1	2	3	4	5	6	7	8	9	10	11	12	13

回想 *huí xiǎng*　recall; recollect　　思想 *sī xiǎng*　thought; thinking
想象 *xiǎng xiàng*　imagine　　　　　　想家 *xiǎng jiā*　homesick

忘

wàng
forget

The upper part of the character comes from 亡, meaning 'to disappear' or 'perish', represented by someone 入 going into a hiding place ㄴ. The addition of the heart radical 心 below reinforces the idea of 'lost mind' or a mind that ceases to act; hence, to forget 忘.

| 忘记 | *wàng jì* | forget | 难忘 | *nán wàng* | unforgettable |
| 健忘 | *jiàn wàng* | forgetful | 遗忘 | *yí wàng* | pass into oblivion |

wáng
king

The character for 'king' 王 was originally a picture of a string of jade beads ⅀ – a luxury only royalty could afford. It has also been interpreted as three horizontal planes 三 (representing heaven, man and earth) connected by a vertical structure ❘, representing the person vested with the power, between heaven and earth, to rule uprightly over man.

一	二	干	王
1	2	3	4

国王   *guó wáng*   king   王宫   *wáng gōng*   palace
王朝   *wáng cháo*   dynasty   王子   *wáng zi*   prince

玉

yù
jade;
gem

As the original symbol of jade beads 王 came to represent the king, a dot 、 was added to form 玉 to continue to refer to jade.

Highly valued as a symbol of excellence and purity, jade may be found in its crude form hidden in rough stone. Hence the saying: 'Jade that has not been chiselled and polished is not an article of beauty.'

一	二	干	王	玉
1	2	3	4	5

美玉　*měi yù*　beautiful jade

玉器　*yù qì*　jade objects

金玉　*jīn yù*　gold and jade; treasures

玉米　*yù mǐ*　corn (maize)

111

guó
country

(Traditional)

Composed of 囗 (boundary), – (land), 口 (mouth) and 戈 (spear), 國 means the land, people and weapons within a boundary – a country. The simplified form of the character retains the boundary, but replaces what's inside with 玉 (jade, representing the king).

| 国歌 | *guó gē* | national anthem | 国内 | *guó nèi* | domestic |
| 出国 | *chū guó* | go abroad | 国外 | *guó wài* | overseas |

金  *jīn*
gold

The early form of the character 金 showed the presence 今 of four gold nuggets ⦂⦂ hidden in the earth 土. In the present form only two nuggets are left 金. When the word is used as a radical 钅, even the two remaining nuggets are gone. However, the proverb reassures us: 'True gold fears no fire.' Only thieves!

ノ	人	仝	今	仐	仐	余	金
1	2	3	4	5	6	7	8

金色 *jīn sè*   golden

金鱼 *jīn yú*   goldfish

现金 *xiàn jīn*   cash

白金 *bái jīn*   platinum

wǎng

net

網

(Traditional)

This character started as a pictograph of a net 网. Along the way, it was cast aside and replaced by the form 網, made up of 糸 (silk) and 罔 (trap) – but without much success. So the early pictograph of the net was taken up again for the modern simplified form, demonstrating that: 'There is a day to cast your nets, and a day to dry your nets.'

| 1 | 2 | 3 | 4 | 5 | 6 |

渔网　*yú wǎng*　fishing net 　　网络　*wǎng luò*　network

网球　*wǎng qiú*　tennis　　　　上网　*shàng wǎng*　use the internet

买

mǎi

buy

買

(Traditional)

The ideograph 買 means to buy – for example, a net 罒 of goods (modified from 网) – and paying for it in cowrie shells 貝. The simplified form is 买.

㇇	㇇	㇈	乛	乑	买
1	2	3	4	5	6

买家   *mǎi jiā*   buyer   购买   *gòu mǎi*   purchase

买卖   *mǎi mài*   trading   收买   *shōu mǎi*   bribe

足

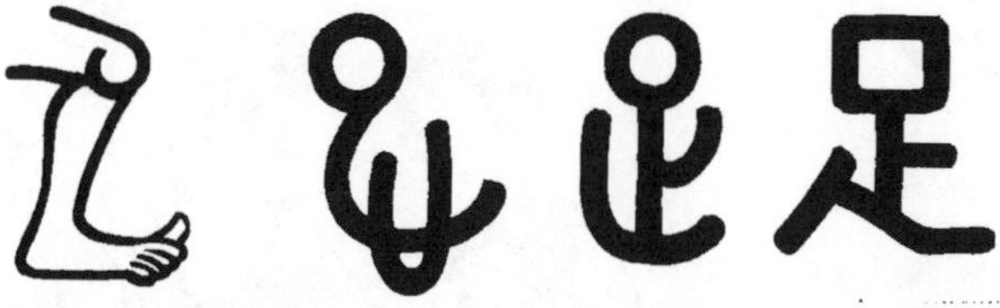

zú

foot

The character 足 depicts the knee-cap ○ over the foot 止. The full circle ○ suggests completion and rest. The modern form 足, signifying the foot at rest, applies to feet in general. And feet are generally at rest, as the illustrations show.

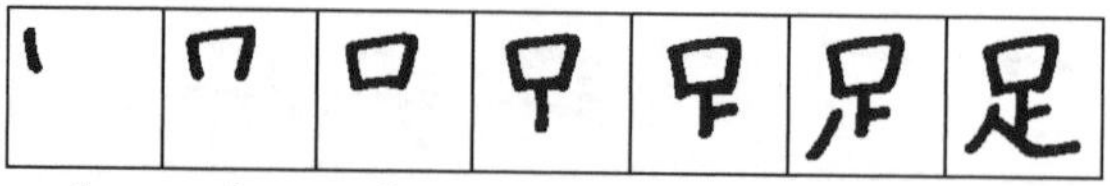

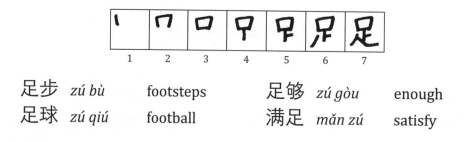

1 2 3 4 5 6 7

足步	*zú bù*	footsteps	足够	*zú gòu*	enough
足球	*zú qiú*	football	满足	*mǎn zú*	satisfy

走 *zǒu* walk

走 走 走

In the early form of the word 走, the upper part 夭 (or 土) represents a man 大 bending his head ノ forward to walk rapidly. The lower part 止 (or 龰) means 'to stop.' This combination of bending and stopping came to describe the action of walking.

一	十	土	才	卡	𤞉	走
1	2	3	4	5	6	7

走路 *zǒu lù*   walk   飞走 *fēi zǒu*   fly away

走开 *zǒu kāi*   go away   逃走 *táo zǒu*   escape; flee

胃

wèi
stomach

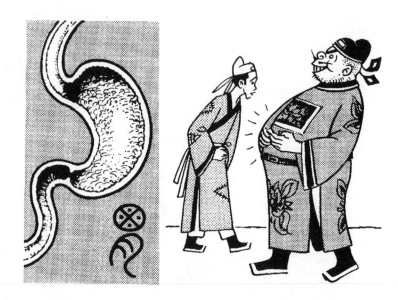

This ideograph combines two pictographs: a pouch filled with rice ⊗, and a piece of flesh 月. Hence the stomach – a fleshy pouch filled with rice. Although a full stomach begets a contented mind, 'Better be hungry and pure than well-filled and corrupt.'

| 肠胃 | *cháng wèi* | stomach; intestine | 胃口 | *wèi kǒu* | appetite |
| 胃病 | *wèi bìng* | stomach trouble | 胃酸 | *wèi suān* | gastric acid |

房 *fáng*
room; house

房 combines 戶 (door) with 方 (square), indicating something squarish with a door, i.e., a house or a room. Looking at a house and a room, one proverb draws the conclusion: 'Even if your dwelling contains a thousand rooms, you can use but eight feet of space a night.'

| 房屋 | *fáng wū* | house; building | 书房 | *shū fáng* | study room |
| 房间 | *fáng jiān* | room | 卧房 | *wò fáng* | bedroom |

写

xiě
write

寫
(Traditional)

寫 **was originally a picture of a magpie** 舄 **under a roof** 宀. **The magpie is a tidy bird with the habit of picking up bright objects and hiding them.** 寫 **therefore suggests setting objects and ideas in order, and by extension, the act of writing.**

丶	冖	冖	写	写
1	2	3	4	5

写信	*xiě xìn*	write a letter	写作	*xiě zuò*	writing
手写	*shǒu xiě*	handwriting	描写	*miáo xiě*	describe; depict

画

huà
painting; drawing

畫

(Traditional)

A painting 畫 is symbolised by the artist's brush 聿 and his picture 田. In the present simplified form 画, the brush has disappeared, but the picture frame 凵 (which came and went over the course of the character's evolution) makes a return.

| 画家 | *huà jiā* | artist; painter | 国画 | *guó huà* | Chinese painting |
| 画室 | *huà shì* | studio | 油画 | *yóu huà* | oil painting |

先 *xiān*
first; before

The upper part of the character is a small plant Ψ growing from the ground —, indicating progress. The lower part is a picture of marching legs. Accordingly, 先 means to advance 㞢 on one's feet ㄦ, i.e., to be first.

ノ	╭	㪯	生	步	先
1	2	3	4	5	6

首先	*shǒu xiān*	first; first of all	祖先	*zǔ xiān*	ancestor
先后	*xiān hòu*	one after another	领先	*lǐng xiān*	to lead

洗

xǐ
wash;
clean

**The water radical 氵 combined with the phonetic 先 (which
also means 'first') gives the word for 'wash' or 'cleanse'.** And
what needs to be cleansed first? According to the proverbial exhortation:
'Cleanse your heart as you would cleanse a dish.'

洗澡　*xǐ zǎo*　take a bath　　　洗手间　*xǐ shǒu jiān*　toilet
洗碗　*xǐ wǎn*　do the dishes　　洗衣机　*xǐ yī jī*　washing machine

马 馬 (Traditional)

mǎ

horse

馬 is a picturesque representation of a rearing horse. The character has since been simplified, losing its eyes and mane. The present character reduces it to three masterly strokes 马 – a skeletal horse, advanced in age but rich in experience, inspiring the proverb: 'The old horse knows the way.'

| 骑马 | *qí mǎ* | ride a horse | 马路 | *mǎ lù* | road |
| 木马 | *mù mǎ* | rocking horse | 马上 | *mǎ shàng* | immediately |

牛

niú

OX; COW

The early form of this character was a pictograph of the ox, characterised by two prominent horns 半. As man's slave for life, the cow or ox has been exploited to the bone for labour, meat, milk, leather, glue, manure, etc. The modern form 牛 does not even spare the poor animal its horn.

ノ	⺦	⺧	牛
1	2	3	4

牛奶 *niú nǎi* cow's milk 　　牛肉 *niú ròu* beef
牛皮 *niú pí* leather 　　　　牛仔裤 *niú zǎi kù* jeans

狗

gǒu
dog

The character for dog fittingly combines the dog radical 犭 (derived from 犬) with the phonetic 句. Counselling against the thoughtless ill-treatment of the underdog, a wise proverb warns: 'In beating a dog, first find out who the owner is.'

小狗	*xiǎo gǒu*	puppy	野狗	*yě gǒu*	wild dog
狗屋	*gǒu wū*	kennel	热狗	*rè gǒu*	hot dog

鱼

yú
fish

魚
(Traditional)

鱼 鱼 鱼 魚 魚 魚 魚

鱼 is a well-preserved pictograph of the fish. The predatory habits of fish give rise to the saying: 'Big fish eat small fish; small fish eat water insects; water insects eat weeds and mud.' The tail of the fish ⺣ proves to be its fiery end, being a form of fire 火, presumably kindled as man prepares to eat some big fish.

ノ	ク	ク	勹	甸	角	鱼	鱼
1	2	3	4	5	6	7	8

钓鱼 *diào yú* fishing   飞鱼 *fēi yú* flying fish
烤鱼 *kǎo yú* grilled fish   人鱼 *rén yú* mermaid

象

xiàng
elephant

This character is a striking image of the elephant, emphasising its trunk and tusks. Elephant tusks are prized by man as a source of ivory, and so elephants have been a target of hunters throughout history. In the words of the proverb: 'The elephant is killed because of its tusks' – valuable possessions can pose a hazard to their owner.

| 大象 | *dà xiàng* | elephant | 象鼻 | *xiàng bí* | elephant trunk |
| 象牙 | *xiàng yá* | ivory | 好象 | *hǎo xiàng* | seem; like |